Asthma

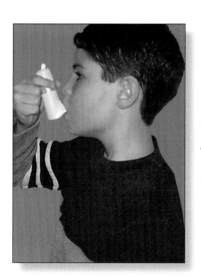

SUSAN DUDLEY GOLD

Expert Review by Vassily Mihailoff, M.D.

Enslow Publishers, Inc.

40 Industrial Road	PO Box 38
Box 398	Aldershot
Berkeley Heights, NJ 07922	Hants GU12 6BP
USA	UK

http://www.enslow.com

Dedicated to Dr. Vassily Mihailoff and the members of Bikers with a Heart, who generously give of their time to cheer young people with chronic disease, and to my nephew, Damon Gray, who excelled in track and football despite his asthma

j616.23?
G563a

Acknowledgments
With thanks to:
Vassily Mihailoff, M.D., for his advice and review of this book.
Kristofer King and his family for sharing their story.
Judi King for sharing family photographs for this book.
Derek Hansen for posing for photographs for this book and to his mother, Valerie King Hansen, for taking them.
Mary Mihailoff; Respironics HealthScan Asthma & Allergy Products; and Pari Respiratory Equipment, Inc., for providing photographs for this book.

Copyright © 2000 by Susan Dudley Gold.
Typography, layout, and setup by Custom Communications, Saco, ME

Library of Congress Cataloging-in-Publication Data
Gold, Susan Dudley.
    Asthma / Susan Dudley Gold.
        p. cm. —— (Health watch)
    Includes bibliographical (p.) references and index.
    Summary: Describes the symptoms, causes, diagnosis, and treatment of asthma, as well as guidelines for living with the disease.
    ISBN 0-7660-1656-0 (hardcover)
    1. Asthma—Juvenile literature. [1. Asthma. 2. Diseases.] I. Title.
    II. Health watch (Berkeley Heights, N.J.)
    RC951.G65 2000
    616.2'38—dc21
                                  00-008222
Printed in the United States of America

10 9 8 7 6 5 4 3 2 1

To Our Readers:
All internet addresses in this book were active and appropriate when we went to press. Any comments or suggestions can be sent by e-mail to Comments@enslow.com or to the address on the back cover.

Illustration and Photo Credits:
© PhotoDisc, Inc.: pp. 12, 14, 17, 25, 26 *top* and *bottom*; © Digital Stock, Corbis Corp.: p. 4; courtesy of Judi King: pp. 6, 35; © Jill K. Gregory: Illustrations, pp. 8, 9, 18; courtesy of Valerie King Hansen, pp. 1, 11; courtesy of Pari Respiratory Equipment, Inc., Midlothian, VA, (800) FAST-NEB: p. 15; © Susan Gold: p. 30; courtesy of Respironics HealthScan Asthma & Allergy Products, Cedar Grove, N.J. 07009: p. 33; courtesy of Mary Mihailoff: p. 39.

Cover Illustrations:
Large photo, courtesy of Mary Mihailoff; illustration, © Jill K. Gregory; inset, courtesy of Respironics HealthScan Asthma & Allergy Products.

Contents

CHAPTER 1

What Is Asthma?   5

CHAPTER 2

Asthma Attack   13

CHAPTER 3

Causes of Asthma   18

CHAPTER 4

Diagnosing Asthma   23

CHAPTER 5

Treating Asthma   29

CHAPTER 6

Living With Asthma   37

Further Reading   40
For More Information   42
Glossary   45
Index   48

OVERBROOK PARK

"I love to play sports," Kristofer King said. "I just have to remember to take my medicine and stick to my schedule."

Chapter 1

What Is Asthma?

Kristofer King was five years old when he developed his first symptoms of **asthma**. "I had a very hard time breathing," Kristofer recalls of his first asthma-related visit to the emergency room. "My oxygen level was so low, the doctors thought the [measuring] device was broken."

The doctors eventually discovered that Kristofer was one of millions of children and adults in the United States who have asthma. "I coughed and vomited a lot," Kristofer said. As a result of his disease, Kristofer has spent many days and nights in the hospital. During a baseball game when he was in the sixth grade, Kristofer had an asthma attack so severe that he landed in the hospital for a week. Like many people with asthma, Kristofer also has a number of **allergies** that cause symptoms such as a stuffy nose or rashes.

Now a freshman in high school, Kristofer has learned to live with asthma. By taking medicine on a regular schedule and avoiding things to which he is allergic, Kristofer

Kristofer King celebrates his fifth birthday.

usually is able to breathe freely and keep his asthma symptoms under control. He plays soccer with his friends, rides his exercise bike each night, and participates in physical education with the rest of his class. In 1996 he went on a white-water rafting trip. He has had only one full-blown asthma attack in the last year.

"I love to play sports," he said. "I just have to remember to take my medicine and stick to my schedule."

Like Kristofer, many people with asthma live full lives that often include strenuous activities. Some even participate in world-class sports competitions. United States President Theodore Roosevelt, who led the Rough Riders during the Spanish-American War in 1898, had asthma from birth. Olympic gold-medal swimmer Amy Van Dyken and outstanding female track-and-field athlete Jackie Joyner-Kersee are among the many famous athletes with asthma.

An Ancient Disease

People have had asthma for more than two thousand years. In 25 B.C. the Roman medical writer Celsus reported that people with asthma make a "whistle" sound because the air they breathe is forced through a narrow passage. A century later, a Greek doctor named Aretaeus described the symptoms of asthma. People with asthma, Aretaeus said, have a hard time breathing, are hoarse, and often have coughing spells. The word asthma is a Greek verb meaning "to pant or to breathe hard."

Wheezing (a whistling sound made during breathing) is the symptom most commonly linked to asthma. Some people with asthma, however, never wheeze at all. Instead, they may cough repeatedly or breathe in short, rapid breaths. They may experience chest tightness. Many people with asthma also have allergies and may not be able to smell or taste very well. Infants who have an asthma flareup may not be able to drink or suck strongly. They may breathe rapidly or have a blue tinge to their skin.

What all these people have in common is that they sometimes have to struggle to breathe. Because of their disease they have trouble inhaling fresh air and exhaling stale air. This is because asthma affects the body's ability to breathe.

Most Efficient Breathing Machine

When you breathe, air is drawn into your nose or mouth, then passes into your throat, goes through your voice box (**larynx**), and enters your windpipe (**trachea**). From there, the air travels through two tubes called the **bronchial tubes**, and into the **lungs**.

If you could look inside a person's neck and chest, you would see what resembles an upside-down tree. The

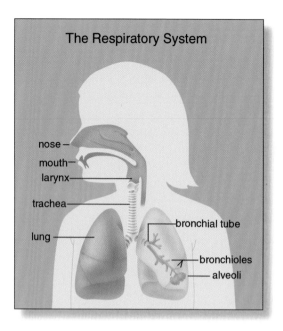

The Respiratory System

nose
mouth
larynx
trachea
lung
bronchial tube
bronchioles
alveoli

The respiratory system controls a person's breathing, bringing in oxygen and carrying out carbon dioxide.

windpipe is the trunk, and the bronchial tubes are the branches. Each bronchial tube splits into thousands of smaller branches called **bronchioles**. A cluster of tiny air sacs, like a bunch of grapes, clings to the end of each bronchiole. Each person has more than 700 million of these air sacs, called **alveoli**. Tiny blood vessels, called **capillaries**, are wrapped around the alveoli. The two lungs, one on each side of the chest, contain the bronchial tubes, the bronchioles, and the alveoli. Together all these parts make up the **respiratory system**.

The air people breathe enters the bronchial tubes and flows through the bronchioles and into the alveoli. Oxygen in this air seeps through the thin covering of the alveoli into the capillaries, where it is absorbed by the blood. The blood carries the oxygen to the rest of the body.

Blood cells also carry carbon dioxide created when the body burns calories. In the lungs, carbon dioxide gas in the blood seeps through the capillaries into the alveoli. When you exhale, carbon dioxide is forced up through the bronchial tubes and out your mouth or nose.

In addition to drawing in air and expelling carbon

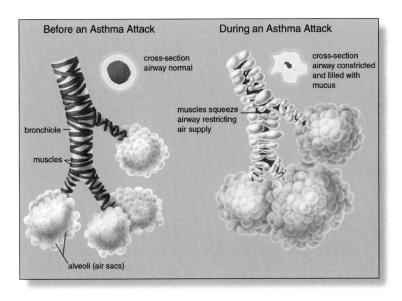

A view of a person's lungs during an asthma attack.

dioxide, the nose has another important role in the respiratory system. Tiny hairs and **mucus** in the nose filter the incoming air and trap germs and tiny dust particles. The nose also moistens and warms the air so that it won't shock the delicate membranes of the bronchial tubes.

Smooth muscle embedded in the walls of the bronchial tubes controls the opening and closing of the airways. This action regulates the amount of air entering the alveoli.

In most people the respiratory system is a very efficient breathing machine. But for people with asthma, the system doesn't work quite right. In asthma, tobacco, **pollen** or some other substance, such as **dust mites** or animal **dander**, irritates the membranes lining the bronchial tubes. The membranes become red and swollen. This narrows the airways leading into the lungs. The muscles in the bronchial tubes tighten and reduce the airway even further. People with asthma can't breathe in enough oxygen and can't exhale enough carbon dioxide. They must work extra hard to breathe. Air being forced through the narrowed airways makes the bronchial tubes vibrate, causing the wheezing sound many people with asthma produce during an attack.

When an asthma patient receives the right kind of treatment, the swelling stops, the muscles relax, and the person can breathe normally again. Unlike some other respiratory illnesses, an asthmatic episode rarely causes permanent damage to the respiratory system. Most people with asthma breathe normally between attacks. New research, however, shows that if a person has repeated asthma attacks, scar tissue may form in the walls of the bronchial tubes. This decreases the width of the airways and can lead to new attacks. That is why it is so important to prevent asthmatic episodes with proper treatment.

A Serious Disease

Even though asthma was first described more than two thousand years ago, many people—including doctors—thought until recently that breathing difficulties were "all in the head" of the patient. For years, most doctors thought asthma was a minor disease, certainly not serious enough to cause death.

Today's medical professionals know differently. Asthma is a serious disease affecting more than 100 million people worldwide. Between 12 million and 15 million Americans have been diagnosed with asthma, and many more suffer from its effects without knowing they have it. Doctors are diagnosing more people, especially children, with the disease each year. In the years between 1980 and 1994, the number of people with asthma doubled. No one is sure why the rate of asthma cases continues to climb.

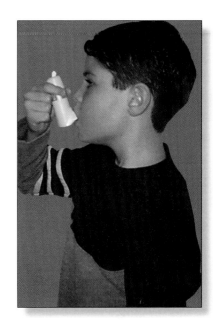

Asthma is a **chronic disease**, which means that a person is likely to have it for a long time. In the United States it affects more children under age seventeen than any other chronic disorder. There is no cure, but proper treat-

Derek Hansen, who has asthma, uses his inhaler. Proper treatment can control asthma symptoms.

ment can control the symptoms of asthma in almost every case. If left untreated, however, asthma can be fatal.

Medical experts say no one should die from asthma. Unfortunately many people do not receive treatment for the illness. Some people don't know they have the disease. Others don't realize how important it is to treat asthma, and they ignore the symptoms. Still others don't have access to proper medical care. As a result, at least five thousand Americans die from asthma each year, and as many as 10 to 15 percent die within the first three hours of an attack. Others suffer from collapsed lungs, fractured ribs, and other major health risks. At the end of the 1970s, the number of asthma deaths in the United States began rising. Today, more than twenty years later, asthma-related deaths are increasing by 8 percent a year.

A beautiful field of flowers can cause itchy eyes, sneezing, and discomfort in someone with asthma.

Asthma is more common in children than in adults, and boys are twice as likely to have the disease as girls. In adults, asthma is equally common in men and women. Though people can be diagnosed with asthma at any age, in the United States 50 to 80 percent develop the disease before age five. Most have allergies to pollen, dust mites, animal dander, certain foods, or other substances.

Asthma has a tremendous impact on the American economy. It is the most common reason why children miss school. Each year, children in the United States are absent from school more than 10 million days due to asthma. Parents who stay home with their sick children cost the nation almost $1 billion in lost time at work. Americans seeking treatment for asthma spend an estimated $5 billion for health care annually.

Chapter 2

Asthma Attack

During an asthma attack the bronchial tubes tighten, and the membranes in the lining of the tubes swell. Glands inside the bronchial lining produce thick mucus that blocks the airways.

People who are having an asthma attack must focus all their efforts on trying to breathe. They may not be able to talk. Many wheeze loudly, gasp, or pant. A person's chest may heave violently, and the neck muscles may move rapidly as he or she desperately tries to get a breath of air. The effort to breathe may leave the asthma patient exhausted. One person said an asthma attack made her feel as if she were drowning.

Kristofer King's first sign of an attack is a bad bout of coughing. Then his chest starts to hurt.

"It's pretty miserable, actually," he says. He has trouble getting enough air into his lungs and is short of breath. He feels weak and tired.

"When it's really bad," he says, "I get panicky."

In many cases a person with asthma who is having

difficulty breathing will spray a medicated mist into his or her mouth through an **inhaler** and then breathe it in. The medication in the mist relaxes the muscles around the bronchial tubes and allows the patient to breathe more easily within minutes.

Need for Immediate Help

Some people, however, may not be able to breathe deeply enough during an attack to use an inhaler. People who experience a severe asthma attack must get help immediately. Usually that means a quick trip to the emergency room of the nearest hospital. During a severe attack a person who does not get treatment right away can stop breathing and die.

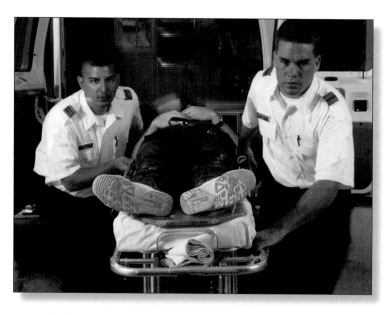

People having an asthma attack may need to make a quick trip to the hospital.

A girl uses a nebulizer to help her breathe more easily.

During Kristofer's first asthma attack, he coughed so hard that he ruptured the blood vessels in his eyes. "It was so severe," said his mother, Judi King, "that the eye doctor thought he had been beaten."

In the hospital, asthma patients are hooked up to a machine called a **nebulizer**, which helps them breathe. A liquid drug is poured into the nebulizer, which transforms the liquid into a mist. Patients inhale the mist through a mouthpiece attached to the nebulizer. The medicated mist relaxes the muscles around the bronchial tubes and opens up the airways. Kristofer has a nebulizer at home, which he uses when breathing becomes difficult.

If people still have trouble breathing, doctors may give them a shot of **adrenaline**. Adrenaline is a substance produced naturally by the body in glands that lie near the kidneys. The glands release adrenaline in response to fear, cold, or shock. This chemical relaxes the muscles in the walls of the bronchial tubes, allowing more efficient breathing. It also raises the blood pressure and speeds up the heart.

Kristofer says an adrenaline shot has an immediate effect on him: "My hands shake and I can't stay still, but it opens up the airways."

Leading Cause of Hospital Stays

Asthma sends more children to the hospital than any other cause. Because children have smaller airways than adults do, their attacks can be more serious. Kristofer misses one to two weeks of school each time he has a severe attack. During that time doctors treat him with various drugs to control his symptoms.

"It stinks," he says. "I'm home for a couple of days, then I'm at the hospital, then I'm home for a couple more days." Despite his absences from school, Kristofer has managed to earn A's and B's by studying at home.

Deaths occur when severe cases of asthma go untreated. In some cases people don't like to admit they have a disease. By ignoring it they hope it will go away. Others believe the myth that asthma is a mental problem. They try to will it away. Unfortunately that approach doesn't work either.

For many people living in poverty in the nation's cities, asthma is too often a fatal disease. Pollution and damp, unsanitary housing expose city dwellers to substances that can trigger asthma symptoms. Too poor to pay for medical care, many people without insurance receive treatment only when they go to an emergency room during an asthma attack. In the 1990s, African-American children living in American cities were twice as likely to die from asthma as white children living in the suburbs.

Even those who have received treatment for asthma in the past may not realize how important it is to continue their treatment. Bobby Williams, a hockey player with the Boston Bruins franchise, died during an asthma attack in

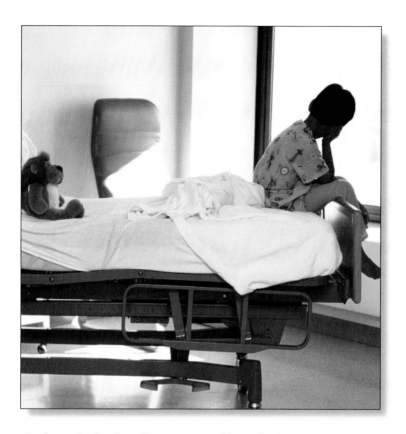

Asthma is the leading cause of hospital stays among American children.

1987. The twenty-three-year-old athlete took medications regularly during hockey season but stopped using them during the summer. One hot day, while working on a roof, Williams suddenly started gasping for breath. He tried to use his inhaler but he couldn't take a breath deep enough to suck in the mist. His coworkers rushed to help him, but Williams died before the ambulance arrived. The amount of pollen in the air—which had bothered Williams in the past—had been exceptionally high that day. Williams's father said the family hadn't realized how serious asthma was.

Chapter 3

Causes of Asthma

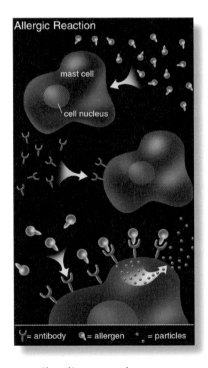

Allergic Reaction

mast cell

cell nucleus

Y = antibody   = allergen   = particles

Antibodies attack allergens, causing chemical reactions that make the airways swell.

Scientists are not exactly sure what causes asthma. Many cases, particularly in children, are linked to allergies. For some reason the respiratory systems of some people overreact to pollen and other substances that cause allergies. These substances are known as **allergens**.

When a person with an **allergy** breathes in an allergen, the body goes on alert. The **immune system**, which normally protects the body by fighting germs and disease, thinks the allergen is an enemy. Immediately, it rounds up **antibodies** to fight the invader. These antibodies rush to surround the allergen. They perch on other cells, called **mast cells**, which release chemicals to try to rid the body of the offending substance. But the chemicals turn out to do more harm than good. One of the chemicals, **histamine**, causes the eyes to itch, the nose to run, and other symptoms seen in the allergy known as hay fever. The chemicals cause the airways, where the allergen has lodged after being inhaled, to swell. This is even worse for the person with asthma. The muscles around the airways tighten, closing down the air passage and making it difficult for the person to breathe. Symptoms of many people with severe allergies become worse each time they breathe in the allergen.

Allergies Run in Families

Allergies usually are inherited from one or both parents. A child whose mother or father has an allergy has a one-in-four chance of inheriting that allergy. If both parents are allergic, most of their children will also have allergies.

Each of us has certain **genes**—tiny units within each cell—that we inherit from our parents. Our genes determine our features: how tall we will be, what color eyes we will have, and, in some cases, which substances will make us have an allergic reaction. Scientists have already found one gene they think is linked to allergies. They continue to search for other genes found only in people with allergies to certain things. By identifying the genes, they hope someday to develop treatments to prevent these allergies.

Although pollen claims the most allergy victims in the suburbs, cockroaches seem to be the culprits in the inner cities. Many people also are allergic to dust, cat dander, and mold spores. Others have food allergies or get severe allergic reactions to certain medications or insect bites. All of these allergies can lead to an asthma attack.

Kristofer has an especially difficult time in the spring, when trees and grass trigger his asthma symptoms, and in the fall, when pollen from ragweed and pigweed fills the air. He is also allergic to dust mites, microscopic insectlike creatures that breed by the thousands in bedding, upholstered furniture, carpets, and curtains.

"In the spring I have to load up on allergy medicine," Kristofer said. Itchy eyes, sneezing, congestion, and a runny nose plague him during those months. When pollen levels are high or neighbors are cutting grass, he may have difficulty breathing as well. When that happens, he increases his medication and sometimes gets a treatment on the nebulizer.

Infections and Pollution

Asthma can also be triggered by infections. A virus can set off the immune system in the same way allergens do. Kristofer's mother tries to keep him away from people who have colds or the flu. Such illnesses may be minor for his friends, but for Kristofer they can trigger an asthma attack. "My mom freaks out every time I cough," says Kristofer.

Air pollution, strong odors, and other factors can irritate the respiratory system and set off an asthma reaction as well. Secondhand smoke can be especially dangerous. Recent studies have shown that as many as 1 million children in the United States whose parents smoke have more frequent asthma attacks than those whose parents don't smoke. Smoke and airborne particles from woodstoves have a similar effect.

Cars that run on gasoline and industrial plants that burn coal or oil release dangerous chemicals into the air. When these chemicals react with sunlight, they create **smog** (also called **ground-level ozone**). This type of air pollution damages healthy lungs and makes asthma even worse. In some cities the smog is so thick that people with respiratory problems have to wear masks to breathe.

Pollution lurks indoors, too. Buildings—well insulated and sealed tight—often trap odors, dust, and other irritants inside. Cleaning solutions, gasoline, paint, perfume, hair spray, and even certain types of food give off strong odors that can trigger an asthma attack in some people.

On-the-Job Dangers

Working with particular materials or being exposed to certain fumes can also lead to asthma. Doctors first noted a link between asthma and certain jobs in the 1700s when people who worked at grain mills began having attacks of breathlessness. Experts have found more than two hundred substances that have resulted in on-the-job asthma. They don't know whether the materials actually cause asthma or just trigger attacks. Among those with **occupational asthma** are veterinarians who have developed allergies to cats or skunk scent, farmers who react to hay, and bakers who are allergic to flour. Hairdressers have been forced to give up their careers when they became allergic to hair sprays and other hair chemicals. In hospitals, health care workers have had to switch to cotton gloves and bandages when their skin reacted to the latex in the plastic versions of these things.

Exercise and Stress

Exercise is one of the most common triggers of asthma attacks, affecting from 70 to 90 percent of those with the disease. During vigorous exercise, people breathe in air rapidly to meet the body's demand for more oxygen. The nasal passages warm the air and add moisture before it enters the bronchial tubes. However, during exercise the amount of air is so great that the nasal passages of people with asthma can't warm and moisturize the air quickly enough. The cold, dry air irritates the bronchial tubes and can trigger an attack. This is especially true when people with asthma exercise in cold climates. Such reactions can be prevented. Many people with asthma exercise regularly without problems. Several have entered and won Olympic events. Among Olympic athletes with asthma are Jim Ryun, winner of the 1,500-meter race; Nancy Hogshead, winner of four medals in swimming; Bill Koch, silver medalist in cross-country skiing; Greg Louganis, gold medalist in diving; and Jackie Joyner-Kersee, medalist in track-and-field events.

For many years doctors believed asthma was caused by mental problems, that it was "all in the head." Today, people know asthma is the result of a physical disease. As with many other diseases, however, asthma can become worse when a person is under stress. A person who is anxious or depressed may find it harder to control the disease.

Chapter 4

Diagnosing Asthma

When Kristofer King first began wheezing and coughing, his mother thought he had bronchitis.

"I knew nothing about asthma," she said.

During one particularly bad coughing bout, Kristofer had so much trouble breathing that his mother rushed him to the emergency room of the local hospital. The health care workers there calmed him down, gave him medicine, and eventually sent the five-year-old home. When Kristofer's symptoms continued, his parents brought him back to the hospital, but the staff there again sent him home.

Finally, on his third trip to the hospital, a nurse tested the amount of oxygen entering Kristofer's lungs. The device registered such a low oxygen level that the nurse thought the machine was broken. A doctor on duty gave Kristofer oxygen, ordered further tests, and had **X-rays** taken of his chest. Based on the test results, the doctor told Kristofer and his family that he had asthma.

Asthma is not always easy to diagnose. People can cough and wheeze from many other causes. Often asthma symptoms are mistakenly blamed on a cold, bronchitis, pneumonia, or other respiratory problem. Cystic fibrosis, an inherited disease that interferes with breathing, can produce asthmalike symptoms. People who have emphysema—a condition that damages the lungs—wheeze and cough, as do people with heart failure or lung **tumors**. Some people have severe allergies but have no trace of asthma. In a few cases a person may have breathed in something that is lodged in the windpipe and causes the wheezing sound associated with asthma. Although wheezing is probably the most common symptom of asthma, some people with the disease never wheeze.

Detective Work

A doctor examining a patient with asthma symptoms is like a detective who sifts through evidence to solve a mystery. First the doctor asks the patient about past medical problems. Of special interest is whether the patient is allergic to anything. The doctor also will want to know what medications the person is using. The doctor explores the family's medical history: Are the patient's parents allergic to anything? Do they have asthma or respiratory problems? Do brothers and sisters also cough and wheeze a lot?

The doctor then records the patient's symptoms: Does the patient cough or wheeze? Does he or she experience

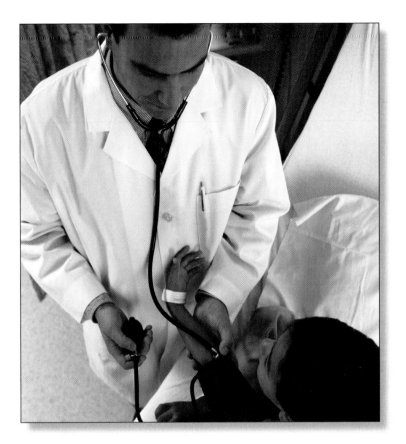

A doctor takes a young patient's blood pressure as part of a thorough physical exam.

tightness in the chest? Suffer from shortness of breath? Have painful sinus infections or a stuffy nose? Have difficulty smelling or tasting? Does the patient have frequent skin rashes or hives?

The doctor also wants to know when the patient has attacks and what triggers them. The patient is asked to describe episodes when breathing is difficult: Is it worse at night? Does it happen on days when there is a lot of pollen in the air? After eating certain foods? When the patient is under stress?

Sometimes a doctor will ask a patient to record in a journal exactly when and how the symptoms occur. After consulting their journal, workers may discover that the problem occurs only when they are at work. This suggests that a substance at the office or factory may be triggering the attacks. A child's journal may reveal that the symptoms are worse at night. That may mean that dust mites in the child's mattress and pillow are causing the problem, or something else in the home may be to blame.

A person may have asthma attacks only at work. For example, fumes at a foundry may trigger asthma attacks in some workers.

Physical Exam

After talking with the patient and family members, the doctor performs a series of tests and examines the patient's body thoroughly. The doctor checks for skin rashes or an inflamed nasal passage. These symptoms can be caused by allergies, which are frequently linked to asthma.

The doctor listens to the patient's breathing to determine whether it is normal. People with asthma often have

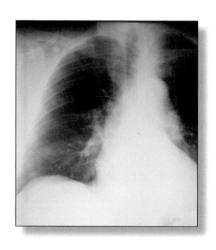

An X-ray of the lungs can show if a patient has pneumonia or other reasons for his or her symptoms.

trouble taking a deep breath without coughing or wheezing. Doctors may take X-rays and order tests to rule out other causes. In Kristofer's case X-rays showed he didn't have pneumonia (an infection of the lungs). X-rays can also reveal a tumor or an object caught in a patient's windpipe.

Perhaps the most important tests for someone thought to have asthma are those that record the patient's breathing pattern. In one test, given only to people who are at least five years old, the patient blows into a machine called a **spirometer**. The spirometer, which is attached to a computer, records the amount of air exhaled and the force used. The readings are compared with those for people without asthma. After inhaling medication designed to open airways, the patient blows again into the spirometer. The medication allows a person with asthma to exhale more air than before. People with other diseases probably won't show any improvement.

Sometimes patients are also tested before and after they exercise. After breathing into the spirometer, patients walk on a treadmill or pedal an exercise bike until they are out of breath. Then they are tested again to see whether they are having trouble breathing. This test is not always conducted because it can be dangerous for some patients.

Other tests measure the volume of a patient's lungs, the amount of oxygen in a patient's blood, and the amount of carbon dioxide in the air a person exhales.

Most patients don't have to take all the tests listed above. Often a doctor can tell that a patient has asthma from the medical history, the physical examination, and the breathing tests.

Allergy Tests

Because allergies trigger asthma attacks in so many people, it is important to find out whether a patient is allergic to anything. Once patients know they are allergic, they can take steps to avoid the substances that give them trouble. One way to identify allergens is to prick a patient's skin and apply a substance that might cause an allergic reaction. This is known as a **prick test**. If the skin near the area where the test allergen is applied swells, turns red, and develops a welt (or bump), the patient is probably allergic to that substance. The larger the area that reacts to the test, the more allergic to the substance the patient is. Doctors have used allergy skin tests for more than one hundred years. Usually they are quite reliable in finding out what substances bother patients.

An **allergist**, a doctor who specializes in allergies, did two series of prick tests to identify Kristofer's allergens. Each time, the doctor pricked Kristofer's arm above the elbow with a series of twenty or more substances. Kristofer had no reaction to the first series—for animal dander and foods. That was a relief, since the family has two cats. The second series—for dust mites, mold, grass, trees, and ragweed—showed dramatic results. Bits of grass produced a large welt on Kristofer's arm. He had similar reactions to most of the other substances in the series.

These tests gave the doctor the information he needed to help Kristofer control his asthma symptoms. Whenever pollen is in the air, Kristofer takes extra medicine. He also tries to avoid the other substances on his allergy list.

Chapter 5

Treating Asthma

Most people who have asthma will have it for life and must be treated regularly. Originally, people thought that children outgrew asthma. More recent research has found that three-quarters of those with asthma will have the disease as long as they live. Some, however, will go through long periods without having any symptoms of the disease.

Most people with asthma can live a fairly normal life and avoid attacks or reduce their severity by taking regular medication. Several medicines are available to treat asthma. The most commonly used asthma drugs are called **beta-agonists**. These drugs contain a type of adrenaline that helps relax bronchial muscles.

Most people take the drug by spraying it into their mouth and inhaling it. Beta-agonists are also available as pills, or as powders that can be inhaled. Children can drink a flavored syrup that contains beta drugs. Patients who can't breathe deeply enough to use an inhaler can absorb beta drugs through the mist created by a nebulizer.

How to Use an Inhaler

1. Exhale.

2. Open mouth and inhale deeply and slowly (three to five seconds) as you spray the mist into your mouth.

3. Hold breath for at least ten seconds.

4. Let air out easily.

5. Wait one or two minutes and repeat.

An inhaler with beta drugs offers quick relief for anyone having trouble breathing. Usually a puff or two frees up the airways within minutes. The effects can last up to six hours. The beta inhaler must be used only as needed. Most doctors don't recommend using it daily over a long period of time. Athletes, however, may need to use the beta spray more frequently to prevent an asthma attack brought on by exercise.

Those who have trouble with timing their breathing to coordinate with spraying can use a spacer. The spacer stores the sprayed drug until the patient breathes it in. People can also use a face mask to make it easier to breathe in the drug.

Also important in asthma treatment are drugs called **corticosteroids**. These steroids are not like the ones that some bodybuilders take to develop muscles. These drugs fight inflammation and reduce swelling of the lining of the bronchial tubes.

Until the 1970s, people with asthma took steroid pills or had steroid shots. Today steroids can be inhaled, just as beta drugs are. This reduces the amount taken at one time and makes it easier for patients to take the right dose. Steroid sprays can take up to three weeks to start working. Some patients use steroid sprays daily to keep their asthma under control.

In serious cases, patients sometimes are given steroid pills or shots, which act faster than steroid sprays in reducing swelling. They can have serious side effects, however, if used over a long period of time. Heavy doses of steroids can interfere with the body's ability to produce its own natural inflammation-fighting steroids. Steroid shots or pills can also raise the blood pressure, increase a person's weight, lead to depression, or cause nervous energy. Because of the side effects of steroids, doctors carefully monitor their use.

Another medicine, often recommended for children, is **cromolyn sodium**. It also helps fight inflammation and reduces swelling. Cromolyn sodium prevents the body from releasing histamine. The medicine has the same chemicals as an herbal remedy (khellin) used thousands of years ago in Egypt for asthma patients. Cromolyn sodium comes in an inhaler for use by people with asthma. It is also used in nebulizers in solution form. It takes three to six weeks to have an effect. Many people with asthma take the drug every day to prevent attacks and to help them breathe more easily. Unfortunately it doesn't work for everyone.

Doctors and patients have to experiment to find out what works best for them. A medicine that works for one patient may have no effect on someone else. Sometimes a medicine may help a patient for months or years and then stop working. People with asthma may go to their family doctor for treatment. Others may consult with an allergist or a **pulmonologist**, a doctor who specializes in asthma and lung diseases.

After seeing an allergist, Kristofer began using a beta spray and a steroid spray twice a day. When Kristofer's asthma started bothering him again, the doctor stopped the beta spray and replaced it with another kind of beta spray, which he also used twice a day. "That kept me out of the hospital and seemed to control my asthma," Kristofer recalled. Then he had an attack. The doctor took him off one spray and replaced it with another, increasing the dosage of both medications Kristofer was taking. For a time Kristofer also had to take steroid pills.

As Kristofer's condition changes, his doctor modifies the drugs he takes. Lately Kristofer has been able to stop taking the steroid pills and has reduced the dosage of one spray. "If it doesn't work," Kristofer said, "you just try something else." His main goal is to avoid having an asthma attack and to stay out of the hospital. That is why he works with his doctor as closely as possible to find a combination that helps him.

Treatment Plan

Most people—85 to 90 percent—have warning signals when they are about to have an asthma attack. This gives them time to take medication, such as that found in an inhaler, to prevent the attack. Shortness of breath is the most common signal that an attack may occur. People with asthma can test their breathing on a simple device called a **peak flow meter**, which looks like an inhaler.

A person using this meter breathes in deeply, then exhales as hard as possible into the device. A built-in scale on the device measures the force of the breath. By recording their breathing in the morning and the evening, people can tell what reading is normal for them. When the force of a breath is less than normal, it is a signal that the person needs to take steps to prevent a full-blown asthma attack. Because of this the peak flow meter is known as an "early warning device."

Doctors often help patients draw up a plan to follow when they feel an attack coming on. Each plan is different, reflecting the needs of the particular patient. Friends, coworkers, and relatives should be aware of the treatment plan so they will know what to do for the person having an attack. Parents and teachers can help children in their care follow the plan designed for them.

Kristofer takes his nebulizer and his medications to school, where the school nurse helps him

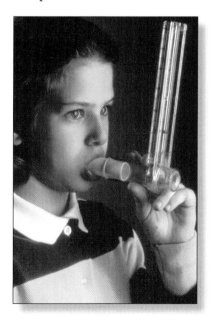

A peak flow meter warns people when they are at risk for an asthma attack and is useful for everyone with active asthma.

with treatments, if necessary. His friends seem to take Kristofer's disease in stride, too, though sometimes they are disappointed when he says he can't go bike riding after an attack.

"They don't treat me any differently," he says. "They're usually understanding." When he sleeps over at a friend's house, he takes the nebulizer with him.

Avoiding Allergens

One way to prevent asthma attacks is to avoid allergens whenever possible. Kristofer's mother covered his mattress and pillow with airtight covers to protect him from dust mites. He tries to stay inside when there is a lot of pollen in the air. People who are allergic to pets are advised to stay away from them. Those with allergies to mold spores and pollen can use dehumidifiers and air filters to keep inside air clean and dry. People with food allergies can avoid eating certain foods.

Of course, people can't always avoid everything that causes an allergy. Molds grow on plants, grass, and leaves outdoors and on food, furniture, and air conditioners indoors. They thrive in basements and other damp areas. Walter Luis, a plant expert at Washington University in St. Louis, Missouri, notes that hundreds of thousands of mold spores can exist in a single cubic meter of air. A person breathes in ten to twelve cubic meters of air every day.

People may still have to go to work or school when the pollen count is high. Laws in many states forbid smoking in public places, but people are still exposed to second-hand smoke in private clubs, homes, and outdoor gathering

Kristofer enjoys skateboarding. From left: Beau King, Kristofer's brother; friend Keith Troester; and Kristofer.

spots. Pollution continues to be a problem in many areas of the country.

People who are allergic to a number of things—many kinds of pollen, for example—can get shots to help reduce their allergies. The injections are called **desensitizing therapy** because they make a person less sensitive to allergens. Over a period of months, the doctor injects the patient with a tiny amount of the substance causing the allergy. The amount of allergen is increased little by little until the patient's body becomes used to the substance and no longer produces antibodies to fight it. The shots work best in children.

In rare cases the shots can be dangerous. Just a tiny amount of allergen can trigger a severe reaction in a few people. Sometimes a person's allergic reaction gets worse each time he or she is exposed to a certain substance. That is why allergy shots are given in a doctor's office, or in some cases in the hospital, so patients can be treated if they have a bad reaction.

There are no shots that make people less allergic to foods. Those with food allergies must avoid eating the foods that give them trouble. That means reading labels carefully and checking with the cook to make sure the recipe doesn't include food that causes allergic reactions.

Precautions During Exercise

Exercise can trigger asthma attacks. Yet some athletes have been so successful in controlling their asthma that they have excelled in their sport.

Athletes with asthma have been able to succeed by carefully preparing for exercise. Before Kristofer jogs or does something strenuous, he inhales his beta spray. This relaxes his bronchial tubes and allows his lungs to get the extra oxygen they need when he's exercising. Doctors urge those with asthma to do warm-up exercises first and take plenty of rest periods. People with asthma are sometimes advised not to exercise in cold weather or when a lot of pollen is in the air.

Exercise is good for people with asthma, just as it is for everyone. It helps build the muscles, strengthens the heart, and increases the body's overall health. It can also raise people's confidence and help them deal better with the stress of having asthma.

Asthma sometimes prevents Kristofer from playing the sports he loves, but not for long. After an attack during a baseball game sent Kristofer to the hospital, he stayed on the sidelines for a while. Now he is playing soccer with his friends after receiving the go-ahead from his doctor.

Chapter 6

Living With Asthma

For Kristofer, the key to coping with asthma lies in following the doctor's orders and then concentrating on things he enjoys.

"I try not to think I have it," he says. "Except when I'm taking my medicine or someone mentions it or I do strenuous activity, I don't really think about having asthma. I just go about my life."

Kristofer uses both beta drugs and steroid sprays on a regular basis. To help him remember to take his medicine, he keeps the bottles and sprays in a particular spot where he can see them easily. He knows how important it is to use the treatments. His latest asthma attack occurred after he missed a couple of doses of medicine.

Guidelines for Living With Asthma

Kristofer's advice for living with asthma is simple:
- Try to control the disease by limiting exposure to allergens and other factors that trigger attacks.

- See the doctor regularly and do whatever he or she tells you to do.
- Take your medicine.
- Try to do things that are fun, like sports.
- Know your limitations.

Another guideline might be to recognize the importance of friends and family. Kristofer's classmates and friends all know about his disease. He carries his nebulizer on the school bus when he needs it at school. His family cheers him on, helps him make special arrangements to visit friends and go on field trips, nurses him through bouts with asthma, and reminds him to take his medicine. They have spent more hours in the hospital emergency room with Kristofer than they care to remember. It helps to have support from friends and family.

A knowledgeable doctor and specialized treatment help, too. For years Kristofer struggled with repeated asthma attacks. At age thirteen, he was finally referred to an allergist who identified the allergens that triggered his attacks. That knowledge and a new regimen of medication have helped keep Kristofer's asthma under control.

"The doctor's done a wicked good job," says Kristofer, a broad smile revealing his affection for the man who helped change his life.

A Special Cheering Section

Dr. Vassily Mihailoff encourages Kristofer to participate in sports and the activities he enjoys. The doctor also knows the importance of a cheering section. In 1996, Bikers with a Heart—a group of motorcyclists formed by

Bikers with a Heart honor Kristofer on his special day. Kristofer is standing in the middle of the front row; Dr. Vassily Mihailoff, founder of the group, is kneeling to Kristofer's left.

Dr. Mihailoff and his friends to cheer youngsters struggling with chronic illnesses—paid Kristofer a visit. Fifty people on motorcycles roared up to Kristofer's doorstep, complete with a police escort. They awarded the astonished Kristofer a grab bag of gifts, his own Bikers with a Heart T-shirt, and lots of encouragement in his efforts to cope with his disease. A special certificate with a Polaroid photo of Kristofer and the bikers proclaimed that day, a Sunday, as Kristofer's special day. Then the group circled the neighborhood, a helmeted and smiling Kristofer riding on the lead motorcycle.

The visit helped lift Kristofer's spirits greatly. It is likely he will have to deal with asthma for the rest of his life, but Kristofer's mother is confident he can handle it. "Kristofer has such a good attitude, it's just amazing," she says.

Further Reading

Booklets

American Lung Association. *American Lung Association's Family Guide to Asthma & Allergies.* New York: Little Brown & Co., 1998.

American Lung Association. *The Asthma Handbook* (ALA #4002). New York: American Lung Association, 1998.

Baldwin, Joyce. *Let's Talk About Asthma: A Guide for Teens* (ALA #1552). New York: American Lung Association, 1993.

Books

DeSalvo, Louise. *Breathless: An Asthma Journal.* Boston: Beacon Press, 1998.

Haas, Dr. François, and Sheila Sperber Haas. *The Essential Asthma Book: A Manual for Asthmatics of All Ages.* New York: Ivy Books, 1998.

Hogshead, Nancy, and Gerald S. Couzens. *Asthma and Exercise.* New York: Henry Holt & Company, 1995.

Hyde, Margaret O., and Elizabeth Forsyth. *Living with Asthma.* New York: Walker & Co., 1995.

Landau, Elaine. *Allergies.* New York: Twenty-First Century Books, 1995.

National Jewish Medical and Research Center. *Asthma Wizard Activity Book.* Denver: National Jewish Center for Immunology and Respiratory Medicine, 1994.

Newman, Gerald, and Eleanor Newman Layfield. *Allergies.* Danbury, Conn.: Franklin Watts, 1992.

Ostrow, William, and Vivian Ostrow. *All About Asthma.* Morton Grove, Ill.: Albert Whitman & Company, 1992.

Parker, Steve. *The Lungs & Breathing,* Rev. ed. Danbury, Conn.: Franklin Watts, 1999.

Plaut, Thomas F., M.D. *One Minute Asthma: What You Need to Know.* Amherst, Mass.: Pedipress, 1998.

Savage, Eileen Dolan. *Winning over Asthma.* Amherst, Mass.: Pedipress, 1993.

Simpson, Carolyn. *Everything You Need to Know about Asthma.* New York: Rosen Publishing Group, 1998.

Ward, Brian. *Breathing! And Your Health.* Danbury, Conn.: Franklin Watts, 1991.

Weiss, Jonathan H., Ph.D. *Breathe Easy: Young People's Guide to Asthma.* Washington, D.C.: American Psychological Association, 1994.

White, T. *Living with Allergies.* Danbury, Conn.: Franklin Watts, 1990.

For More Information

The following is a list of organizations and newsletters that deal with asthma and allergies. Some have Web sites, too.

Organizations

American Academy of Allergy, Asthma, and Immunology
611 E. Wells St., Milwaukee, WI 53202-3889; (414) 272-6071, (800) 822-2762

American College of Allergy, Asthma, and Immunology
85 W. Algonquin Rd., Suite 550, Arlington Heights, IL 60005; (847) 427-1200

American Lung Association
1740 Broadway, New York, NY, 10019-4374; (800) 586-4872 or (212) 315-8700

Asthma and Allergy Foundation of America
1233 Twentieth St. NW, Suite 402, Washington, D.C. 20036; (800) 7-ASTHMA or (202) 466-7643; <http://www.aafc.org>

Allergy and Asthma Network/Mothers of Asthmatics Inc.
2751 Prosperity Ave., Suite 150, Fairfax, VA 22031; (800) 878-4403 or (703) 641-9595

National Asthma Education and Prevention Program, National Heart, Lung and Blood Institute
P.O. Box 30105, Bethesda, MD 20824; (301) 592-8573

National Institute of Allergy and Infectious Diseases
31 Center Drive, MSC 2520, Bldg. 31, Rm. 7A50,
Bethesda, MD 20892-2520. A division of the
National Institutes of Health; (301) 496-5717;
<http://www.niaid.nih.gov>

National Jewish Medical and Research Center
1400 Jackson St., Denver, CO. 80206
(303) 388-4461, Lung Line (800) 222-LUNG

Newsletters

Air Currents. Division of Glaxo, P.O. Box 6577, West
Caldwell, NJ 07007-6577;
<http://www.asthmacontrol.com/aircurrents.html>

Asthma and Allergy Advocate. American Academy of
Allergy, Asthma, and Immunology, 611 E. Wells St.,
Milwaukee, WI 53202

Asthma Update. David C. Jamison, Publisher,
123 Monticello Ave., Annapolis, MD 21401;
<http://www.healthline.com/articles/hl9607dh.htm>

The MA Report. Asthma and Allergy Network/Mothers
of Asthmatics Inc., 2751 Prosperity Ave., Suite 150,
Fairfax, VA 22031, (800) 878-4403

Telephone Hot Lines

Asthma and Allergy Foundation Patient Information
Line, (800) 7-ASTHMA. Information, videos, and
doctor referrals.

Asthma Information Line, (800) 822-ASMA.
Information available twenty-four hours a day.

Lung Line, (800) 222-LUNG. Operated by the National
Jewish Medical and Research Center.

Internet Resources

<http://allergy.mcg.edu>
Allergy, Asthma & Immunology Online, operated by American College of Allergy, Asthma & Immunology.

<http://hsc.virginia.edu/cmc/tutorials/asthma/asthma1.html>
Asthma tutorial by the Children's Medical Center, University of Virginia. View a lung, meet children who have asthma, and listen to an asthma attack.

<http://www.aaaai.org>
Operated by American Academy of Allergy, Asthma & Immunology. Check out the National Allergy Bureau Report, with pollen forecasts for U.S. cities.

<http://www.aanma.org>
Operated by Asthma and Allergy Network/Mothers of Asthmatics Inc. Information and doctor referrals.

<http://www.e-asthma.com>
Facts on asthma and allergies, a listing of famous people with asthma, tips on managing asthma, and information on medications are provided.

<http://www.lungusa.org>
Operated by the American Lung Association.

<http://www.nhlbi.nih.gov>
Operated by the National Heart, Lung and Blood Institute Information Center.

<http://www.nj.com/yucky>
An explanation of the respiratory system. Part of "Your Gross & Cool Body" on the Yucky Bug World site.

<http://www.njc.org>
By National Jewish Medical and Research Center. Check out the "Med Facts" page.

Glossary

adrenaline—A substance produced by the body that raises the blood pressure and speeds up the heart, enabling a person to respond quickly to an emergency; also relaxes the bronchial tubes for more efficient breathing.

allergen—A substance that produces a reaction in an allergic person.

allergist—A doctor who specializes in treating allergies.

allergy—An overreaction by the immune system to substances such as dust, pollen, foods, or animal dander; usually the person sneezes, coughs, or has difficulty breathing.

alveoli—Tiny air sacs found at the end of each bronchiole.

antibodies—Cells produced by the immune system that fight off germs or foreign matter entering the body.

asthma—A chronic disease that interferes with breathing; often linked to allergies.

beta-agonists—Drugs that contain a type of adrenaline that helps relax the bronchial muscles.

bronchial tubes—Two tubes that lead from the trachea to the lungs and through which air travels.

bronchioles—Thousands of thin branches at the end of the bronchial tubes.

capillaries—Tiny blood vessels that connect the arteries and the veins.

chronic disease—A disease that lasts a long time, usually for the life of the patient.

corticosteroids—Drugs that fight inflammation and help reduce swelling.

cromolyn sodium—A drug that reduces swelling and prevents the body from releasing histamine.

dander—Flakes of skin from an animal that often cause allergies.

desensitizing therapy—Shots injected to reduce a patient's allergic reaction to a particular substance.

dust mite—A microscopic insectlike creature found in dust; it lives mainly in pillows, mattresses, upholstered furniture, and carpets.

genes—Tiny units within each cell that determine a person's features.

ground-level ozone—*See* smog.

histamine—A chemical released by the body in response to a foreign substance; causes the eyes to itch, the nose to run, and other coldlike symptoms.

immune system—The system that defends the body against germs and disease.

inhaler—A device that sprays a medicated mist that can be breathed in by a person with asthma.

larynx—The upper part of the respiratory system that contains the voice box, or vocal cords.

lungs—The two body organs where oxygen and carbon dioxide are exchanged during breathing.

mast cells—Cells that watch over the body's tissues and summon antibodies to fight off germs and foreign substances; they release chemicals to help destroy invaders.

mucus—A liquid substance that coats and protects the nose, throat, and bronchial tubes; too much mucus can interfere with breathing.

nebulizer—A machine that changes a liquid into a medicated mist; it helps people who are having trouble breathing, including those who have asthma.

occupational asthma—Asthma that occurs as a result of working with or being exposed to certain materials on the job.

peak flow meter—A small device that measures the force of a person's breath.

pollen—A fine powder released by plants that causes allergies in some people.

prick test—A test in which small amounts of allergens are applied to a patient's skin to find out which ones cause an allergic reaction.

pulmonologist—A doctor who specializes in lung diseases.

respiratory system—The parts of the body that control breathing, including the lungs, trachea, larynx, and bronchial tubes.

smog—Air pollution caused when sunlight reacts with chemicals given off by coal- and oil-burning plants and by cars and trucks.

spirometer—A machine that measures how efficiently a person is breathing.

trachea—The windpipe; a tube connecting the larynx to the bronchial tubes.

tumor—A collection of dividing cells that clump together to form a mass.

X-ray—A picture taken of the inside of the body by using electromagnetic waves.

Index

adrenaline, 15, 29
allergens, 18, 19, 20, 28, 34–35, 37, 38
allergies, 5, 7, 12, 18–19, 20, 21, 24, 26, 28, 34, 35, 36
allergist, 28, 32, 38
alveoli, 8, 9
antibodies, 18–19, 35
Aretaeus, 7
asthma
   attacks, 5, 6, 10, 11, 13–17, 20–21, 21–22, 25, 26, 28, 29, 30, 31, 32, 33, 34, 36, 37, 38
   causes of, 5, 9–10, 12, 18–22
   cost of, 12
   diagnosis of, 11, 23–28
   environmental effects on, 16, 20–22, 34–35
   symptoms of, 5, 6, 7, 11, 16, 19, 20, 23, 24, 25, 26, 28, 29
   treatment of, 10, 11, 12, 14, 16, 19, 20, 29–36, 37, 38
beta-agonists, 29–30, 31, 32, 36, 37
Bikers with a Heart, 38–39
bronchial tubes, 7, 8, 9, 10, 13, 14, 15, 22, 31, 36
bronchitis, 23, 24
Celsus, 6
corticosteroids, 30–31, 32, 37
cromolyn sodium, 31
cystic fibrosis, 24
desensitizing therapy, 35
dust mites, 9, 11, 20, 26, 28, 34
emphysema, 24
exercise-induced asthma, 22, 27, 30, 36
genes, 19

heredity, 19, 24
histamine, 18, 31
Hogshead, Nancy, 22
immune system, 18, 20
infections, 20, 25, 27
inhaler, 14, 17, 29, 30, 31, 33
Joyner-Kersee, Jackie, 6, 22
King, Judi, 15, 20, 23, 34, 39
King, Kristofer, 5–6, 13, 15, 16, 20, 23–24, 27–28, 32–34, 35, 36–39
Koch, Bill, 22
Louganis, Greg, 22
Luis, Walter, 34
lungs, 7, 8, 9, 11, 13, 21, 23, 24, 26, 27, 32, 36
medication, 4, 5, 6, 14, 15, 16, 17, 20, 23, 24, 27, 28, 29, 30, 31, 32, 33, 37, 38
Mihailoff, Dr. Vassily, 38–39
nebulizer, 15, 20, 29, 31, 33–34, 38
occupational asthma, 21–22, 26
Olympics, 6, 22
peak flow meter, 33
pneumonia, 24, 27
prick test, 28
respiratory system, 8–10, 18, 20
Roosevelt, Theodore, 6
Ryun, Jim, 22
smog, 21
spacer, 30
spirometer, 27
stress, 22, 25, 36
treadmill, 27
Van Dyken, Amy, 6
Williams, Bobby, 16–17
X-ray, 23–24, 26, 27

11/01